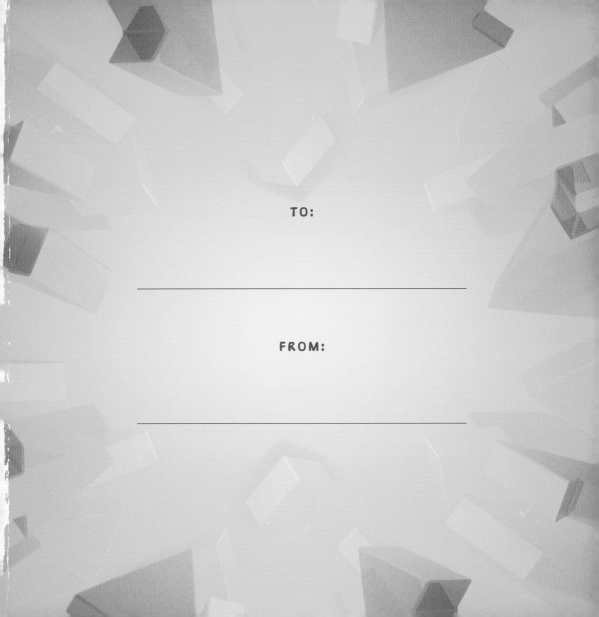

TO:

_____

FROM:

_____

"FOR FAST–ACTING RELIEF, TRY SLOWING DOWN."

-LILY TOMLIN

STRESS
IS A CHOICE

10 RULES TO SIMPLIFY YOUR LIFE

BY DAVID ZERFOSS

"LIFE IS
REALLY SIMPLE,
BUT WE INSIST ON MAKING IT COMPLICATED."
-CONFUCIUS

Introduction

Several years ago while listening to my pastor give a Sunday sermon, he spoke about how life is made up of a series of choices. It made me realize that my hectic professional and personal life was of my choosing. Therefore, a life of stress had become my choice.

Many of us hurry through life going from one place to the next, focused on conquering the next mountain, making the next deal, running the next errand, and believing we will never have enough time to do all the things we need to get done. Yet, there is all the *time in the world if we just realize that we are the creators of this life we choose to live. That's right. **Life is a series of choices and being free from stress is one of those choices.***

Whether your business life is overly complicated or your personal life (or both), you have chosen this current system of chaos. The world is a tantalizing swirl of getting the next "fix," tempting us to fit more and more things, people and processes into our lives, personally and professionally. And because we are so busy being busy, it's easy to be lured into the fray, with our lengthy to-do lists. Yet, the greatest achievements have often come from the simplest of ideas and in the simplest forms.

*To experience a simplified life, **we first have to learn to slow down long enough to see through all the clutter. We need to*** *realize that we are powerful magnets that attracted this life to ourselves—no matter what— good or bad.*

After you read through the 10 Rules to Simplify Your Life, *my wish for you is that you commit to simplify and enroll others for support. Take out a blank sheet of paper and create the life you truly want to live—with less stress and complexity—one that is anchored by a clear sense of your unique and simple purpose.*

Yours for Success,

David Zerfoss

Copyright © 2011 by David Zerfoss

Published by Simple Truths, 1952 McDowell Road,
Suite 300, Naperville, Illinois 60563

Simple Truths is a registered trademark.

8   *Printed and bound in the United States of America.*
ISBN 978-1-60810-132-0

www.simpletruths.com
Toll Free 800-900-3427

Book Design: Vieceli Design Company, West Dundee, Illinois

04 WOZ 12

Table of Contents

RULE #1

SPOT THAT
SPROUT

"Enjoy the little things in life, for one day you may look back and realize they were the big things..."
– ROBERT BRAULT

M

any of us seem to have an endless to-do list. But does all that rushing around stop us from seeing the big picture? Taking a moment to step back from our day-to-day schedules can help us simplify our lives...and maybe even help us to identify what we are missing to keep us energized and fulfilled...

12

"THE ESSENTIAL QUESTION IS NOT, 'HOW BUSY ARE YOU?' BUT 'WHAT ARE YOU BUSY AT?'"

-OPRAH WINFREY

- Run kids to practice
- Get groceries
- Get oil change
- Meditate

Mary kept up a constant and hectic schedule of work travel. It kept her metabolism and adrenaline high. Add this to the fact that she was keeping up with two very active, triple sports-playing teenage sons, which meant there was not much time to think about "simplifying." Besides, simple lives were what other people wanted to have. She was very content. She was busy being busy.

During one business trip out west, she traveled with one of her company's sales representatives. His name was Bob and he was quite up in years. Mary often wondered why Bob continued to work at such a late age in life and chose to keep such a size-able, multi-state territory.

13

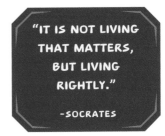

"IT IS NOT LIVING
THAT MATTERS,
BUT LIVING
RIGHTLY."

–SOCRATES

This particular trip they were traveling on an especially long car route visiting customers throughout New Mexico and then on to Colorado. After driving several hours through sparsely populated, very dry and rocky terrain without even a single traffic light in sight for miles, Bob looked over to her and said, **"Are you overwhelmed by the vastness of the landscape and wondering when will it ever end?"** "Yes," she replied. "How did you know what I was thinking?" Bob explained that through his many years of traveling this route, everyone who traveled with him felt the very same thing. Then, Bob went on to share a profound rule with Mary about simplifying.

Bob explained to her that we all can choose to easily get lost in and feel overwhelmed by our surroundings. **"Do you see that**

14

little tree sprouting up there ahead among all those large rock formations?" Bob asked. Mary strained her eyes but could not find what he was seeing. As they got closer, Bob pointed out the small sprouting tree he had seen when it was far off in the distance.

Bob shared with Mary that he handles these long drives through hundreds of miles of vast terrain by looking for the little things among the overwhelming, complex landscape. He doesn't focus

"LOOK FOR WHAT'S MISSING. MANY ADVISORS
CAN TELL A PRESIDENT HOW TO IMPROVE
WHAT'S PROPOSED OR WHAT'S GONE AMISS.
FEW ARE ABLE TO SEE WHAT ISN'T THERE."

-DONALD RUMSFELD

on just seeing what is all around him, but rather he chooses to look for what he might just be missing.

He continued on his drive, merrily searching and pointing out more little things hiding along the way.

As you go about your day, are you letting yourself become overwhelmed by the vast amount of things in your life? Choose to live by one of Bob's rules, and spot that sprout you might otherwise be missing.

16

"IT'S NOT WHAT YOU LOOK AT THAT MATTERS, IT'S WHAT YOU SEE."

-HENRY DAVID THOREAU

SOME QUESTIONS
TO ASK YOURSELF:

→ What's missing in your life?

→ Are you spending too much time on things that don't really matter?

→ What's the "sprout" you need to focus on?

RULE

CARVE OUT TIME

"PAT'S"

"I learned that we can do anything, but we can't do everything... at least not at the same time. So think of your priorities not in terms of what activities you do, but when you do them. Timing is everything."

—DAN MILLMAN

L*ife can become very full very fast. If we first block off time for who and what is most important in our lives, it can actually free us up to really focus on all the rest.*

22

"THE KEY IS NOT TO PRIORITIZE
WHAT'S ON YOUR SCHEDULE, BUT
TO SCHEDULE YOUR PRIORITIES."

—STEPHEN COVEY

I've had the pleasure of getting to know Joe Gibbs, the three-time Super Bowl championship coach and three-time NASCAR® championship team owner. You can say Joe leads a very active life —one full of things to do and people to see—whether he's on the racetrack or on the football field.

One day, I got a glimpse into one of the rules Joe lives by. It's something he carves out only after time spent in a personal relationship with God.

And that's his family time. And in this instance, I'll refer to it as "Pat's Time."

As with all busy executives or famous people, in order to get on Joe's schedule, you have to go through his personal assistant

23

"GOOD THINGS HAPPEN
WHEN YOU
GET YOUR
PRIORITIES
STRAIGHT."

-SCOTT CAAN

24

and you have to want him on a date not already marked out as "Pat's Time."

What's Pat's time? Pat is Joe's wife. As I mentioned earlier, first is Joe's time with God, second comes his time with family. Everything else comes after those first two. Many people may know Joe as a religious man. Well, I can tell you, he's also religious about "Pat's time." It's as simple as that. If you want him for something, at best it will be number three in priority.

You've got to respect a man who lives by simple rules and is so true to his convictions. No matter how

25

> **"SUCCESS IS ONLY ANOTHER FORM OF FAILURE IF WE FORGET WHAT OUR PRIORITIES SHOULD BE."**
>
> **-HARRY LLOYD**

busy life gets for this world-renowned coach and leader, he has his priorities straight in life. He chooses to carve out what's truly important in his life, and in a particular order he feels is most appropriate.

Do you have an order for the priorities in your life or is everything in competition with each other? Choose to carve out some "Pat's time" in your life (whatever this may mean for you). You just may find that it's simply the best time of your life.

"IN A WAY, I HAVE SIMPLIFIED MY LIFE BY SETTING PRIORITIES."

−KAREN DUFFY

SOME QUESTIONS
TO ASK YOURSELF:

→ Do you have a sequence for your competing priorities?

→ Who's your "Pat"?

→ Is she/he on your calendar before all the "to-dos"?

RULE # 3

REDUCE THE NUMBERS

"You have succeeded in life when all you really want is only what you really need."

— VERNON HOWARD

In this world of instant gratification and unlimited choices, we often find ourselves surrounded by mountains of things—furniture, knick-knacks, toys (for children and adults), tools, clothes and so on. Are all these things bringing us real joy and happiness or prohibiting us from seeing what really matters? It's amazing what simple rules we can re-learn when we open our eyes to children at play.

30

"CHILDREN WILL NOT REMEMBER YOU FOR THE MATERIAL THINGS YOU PROVIDED BUT FOR THE FEELING THAT YOU CHERISHED THEM."
-RICHARD L. EVANS

With the pace of the world today, we are often moving so fast that we don't pause to consider what we really need. Are all these things in our lives adding value or just adding clutter to both our surroundings and our lives? Are they complementing our life or complicating it? With each additional thing, often comes additional stress—how to use it, where to put it and ultimately how to pay for it.

Looking back on your early childhood, what intrigued and interested you? For many of us, it was the joy of spending time outdoors. One day I had the pleasure of visiting the Niederman Family Farm in Hamilton, Ohio. The Niedermans have been in farming for many generations. Farming life is so important to them that they open up their home, their land and their barns to folks to come experience what farm life is like. Among other events at the farm, each October they create a giant corn maze for children and adults to wander through day or night by flashlight.

> "ELIMINATE PHYSICAL CLUTTER. MORE IMPORTANTLY, ELIMINATE SPIRITUAL CLUTTER."
>
> -TERRI GUILLEMETS

This past year they were digging out an area for a new addition to their corn maze attraction. A large pile of dirt was placed off to the side until, in true farming fashion, they could determine how they could make good use of it somewhere else on the farm. However, before they got to taking care of that pile of dirt, they found themselves at the opening day of the corn maze. To their surprise, not only was the corn maze itself the usual hit, but children immediately gravitated to that large dirt pile. Kids were running up and sliding down this uninten- tional playing field. There were no blinking lights, no electronics, no sound effects. Just the sound of laughter and fun filled the autumn air as kids were doing what kids do—being imaginative and seizing the moment.

"MEANING DOESN'T LIE IN THINGS. MEANING LIES IN US. WHEN WE ATTACH VALUE TO THINGS THAT AREN'T LOVE— THE MONEY, THE CAR, THE HOUSE, THE PRESTIGE—WE ARE LOVING THINGS THAT CAN'T LOVE US BACK."
-MARIANNE WILLIAMSON

33

As adults, we often find ourselves acquiring more and more things for ourselves and our children—whether it's the next great video game, cell phone, computer, or the latest, hot new toy. As we add more and more material things into our lives, we often forget not only what's most important, but also what it feels like to be childlike—to truly experience life in the moment and therefore be more carefree.

When we focus on what really matters, on what we and our children really "need," life becomes a whole lot simpler—and something as simple as a dirt pile suddenly becomes a whole lot of fun again!

"REDUCE THE COMPLEXITY OF LIFE BY ELIMINATING THE NEEDLESS WANTS OF LIFE, AND THE LABORS OF LIFE REDUCE THEMSELVES."

-EDWIN WAY TEALE

SOME QUESTIONS
TO ASK YOURSELF:

➔ How much is enough?

➔ Where and what can you de-clutter in your life?

➔ Got dirt?

RULE #4

GO FORWARD BY GOING
BACKWARD

"The farther backward you can look, the farther forward you are likely to see."

— WINSTON CHURCHILL

There are many books on the market that teach us how to "be in the present moment." Yet, first we must learn to visit the future. How might our present lives take on new meaning if we think backward from what we envision from the future?

38

"WHEN IT COMES TO THE FUTURE, THERE ARE THREE KINDS OF PEOPLE: THOSE WHO LET IT HAPPEN, THOSE WHO MAKE IT HAPPEN, AND THOSE WHO WONDER WHAT HAPPENED."

-JOHN M. RICHARDSON, JR.

The best way to plan ahead and reduce stress is to "go backward."

That's right. I said, "Go forward by going backward." You see, to create a powerful life or supercharge your business, you have to experience your future right now. See it, feel it, be in it. Then, go backward to the present.

I'm not proposing that we all become psychics or enlist their help to foretell our future. We don't need others to tell us our future. **We each have the power to see the future we want to achieve.** By envisioning your future now, you can make an action plan for how to get there from the present.

When I was a young child growing up in a very small town in

39

"MY INTEREST IS IN THE FUTURE BECAUSE I AM GOING TO SPEND THE REST OF MY LIFE THERE."

-CHARLES F. KETTERING

rural Pennsylvania, I worked on the family farm as well as other farms and went to school at a one-room school house. (Believe it or not, one-room school houses still existed when I was a kid.) After walking to school each day, no matter what the weather, I had the opportunity to learn at my own pace. This open classroom style allowed this young first-grader to also hear the teacher teaching second-grade and third-grade lessons as well. This environment helped me to develop a thirst for learning.

Although my family had very limited means and my mom sewed all of my clothes, I sat in that simple one-room school house and envisioned a bold future for myself. I saw a successful businessman, reading and learning from as many books as I ever wanted, and leading and motivating others.

41

> "LOSERS LIVE IN THE PAST. WINNERS LEARN FROM THE PAST AND ENJOY WORKING IN THE PRESENT TOWARD THE FUTURE."
>
> —DENIS WAITLEY

Thanks to wonderful teachers and that one-room school house's open-learning environment, I went on to graduate from college.

My career path took me to various positions within the petroleum, marine and outdoor recreational vehicle industry and later to become president of a major U.S. division of a multi-national outdoor power equipment company.

Wherever you are in your life and career, you have the power to envision your future. Make a bold declaration and take action in the present to make it happen.

The young boy named David who sat in that one-room school house in homemade clothes, is living proof that if you set your mind to it, you can do it.

Go forward by going backward.

SOME QUESTIONS
TO ASK YOURSELF:

➔ What future did you once dream for your life?

➔ Where are you now?

➔ What is the "Bold Declaration" you can state today to make your desired future a reality?

"LIFE MUST BE UNDERSTOOD
BACKWARD;

BUT...IT MUST BE LIVED

FORWARDS."

-SOREN KIERKEGAARD

RULE # 5

LEAVE THE PAST BEHIND

*"I like the dreams of the future
better than the history of the past."*

— THOMAS JEFFERSON

*W*ithout realizing it, we often carry something around with us everywhere we go. We bring it out in our conversations and it shows up in our attitudes. It never really existed, yet its power lives among us and keeps us from moving forward.

48

"FOR TIME AND THE WORLD DO NOT STAND STILL. CHANGE IS THE LAW OF LIFE. AND THOSE WHO LOOK ONLY TO THE PAST OR THE PRESENT ARE CERTAIN TO MISS THE FUTURE."

-JOHN F. KENNEDY

If you listen to people talk throughout the day, and put a "tick" mark into whether their conversations take place in the Future, in the Present or in the Past, where would you guess most conversations draw from?

The answer is the Past.

Some of us go everywhere with our past and therefore with stress in tow. Why do we do it? It's familiar to us. It's that warm and fuzzy bag of stories we like to take out and share with our family, friends and co-workers. This comfortable past is often our "best friend." It's who and what we know best. It's like a worn-out, easy chair or an old pair of shoes that fits us and feels just right.

And it's the main thing that often keeps us from our desired, incredible Future.

When people talk or think of their past, it seems to take on the characteristics of a real life being. **The Past cannot breathe, talk, think or do.** However, it is very, very powerful and can take over our future, if we let it. It's like the sirens on the shore, luring you into the rocks over and over again. Focusing on the Past will certainly limit your choices for the Future.

> "I'VE GOT MY FAULTS, BUT LIVING IN THE PAST IS NOT ONE OF THEM. THERE'S NO FUTURE IN IT."
>
> -SPARKY ANDERSON (MAJOR LEAGUE BASEBALL COACH)

For a lot of people, I know the Past holds a lot of horrible childhoods, abusive marriages, financially draining job losses and so on. No matter how painful it may have been, we often choose to

50

not let go of this difficult, yet "cozy" Past. Yet, to get on with our Future and simplify our lives, we have to choose to make a clean break.

There's an engaging Peanuts® cartoon where Lucy is apologizing to Charlie Brown for missing a fly ball during a baseball game. She's sorry she missed the fly ball and says it's because she started remembering all the others she missed. **"The Past got in my eyes,"** she says.

Many of us know someone who is very "reason-able," meaning they have very good reasons about why they can't move forward in life. Take for instance a person who has endured multiple bad relationships or marriages. They are certain that because of these relationships they're stuck in the terrible spot they are today. Yet,

"NO MAN IS RICH ENOUGH TO BUY BACK HIS PAST."

-OSCAR WILDE

isn't it hard to watch them as they once again are attracted to the same type of person with whom they just ended a contentious relationship?

Carrying the Past forward to the Future will only provide us with incremental change in our lives. "Unreason-able" people make a choice to create transformational breakthroughs – without "reason-able" ties to the Past.

Each of us has a powerful choice. We have the ability to create our own, simplified future by starting with a blank sheet of paper.

Choose to leave your Past behind and begin living a life filled with new possibilities!

SOME QUESTIONS
TO ASK YOURSELF:

→ How has holding on to your past put limits on your future?

→ What might you need to leave behind or let go of in order to move forward into the future?

→ Is there a situation or a conversation from the past that you need to deal with in the present in order to move on to your future?

RULE #

CHOOSE TO BE A VICTOR

"Life is the sum of all your choices."

— ALBERT CAMUS

*O*ne of the most powerful medicines in the world is "choice." We can choose our attitude, how we react to situations, and with whom we want to share our lives. When illnesses or situations threaten to disrupt our

56

lives, it's our choice to throw in the towel and become a victim or stand and fight, no matter what the out-come— living the life we have as a victor.

"NOTHING IS IMPOSSIBLE. WITH THE RIGHT ATTITUDE, YOU CAN DO ANYTHING YOU WANT."

-MINNIE DRIVER

No matter what your circumstances in life, you have a choice in the matter. You, yourself and the person in the mirror. Get it?

How can this be when there are so many horrific cases of past circumstances in so many lives? All kinds of things happen in life. People do things to us, we do things to people, accidents happen, people come into our lives, people go out of our lives. We choose to let these things and people enter our lives or stay in our lives. We also choose our attitude toward them.

When you cease having a choice, you become a "victim." Whether it's the changing economy, difficult relationships, or a life-changing accident or illness, we possess the strongest mechanism there is to create a breakthrough: the power of choice. We

57

choose how we react, what we think about and what we become—no matter what our surroundings or circumstances. We also choose how we want others to perceive us, acting and speaking accordingly.

In the fall of 2001, I awakened early one morning to get ready to spend the day at an industry trade show. **While shaving, I noticed a lump on the side of my neck. It was not there the day before.** I was not feeling ill and in fact, I had just had a physical 30 days earlier, with a healthy diagnosis.

As soon as I got back into town a few days later, I called my family doctor. After explaining my situation, I got an appointment right away. My family doctor took immediate action and sent me to a specialist. After a series of many tests, the diagnosis was lymphoma. That profoundly confronting word—Cancer—had just entered my life.

It was just a few weeks before the Christmas holidays and the oncologist asked if I would like to wait to begin treatments at the start of the New Year. In my normal fashion of attacking a problem head on, I said, "Let's get to work on beating this thing–right now." To be quite frank, I was scared to death. After living a very fast-paced life and conquering many challenges, there is nothing that compares to the confronting nature of the "C" word and the fact that your life may

> "ATTITUDE IS A LITTLE THING THAT MAKES A BIG DIFFERENCE."
>
> -WINSTON CHURCHILL

soon be over. A series of questions start reeling in your mind: Will you be there to see all your grandchildren be born, graduate, and get married?

> "THE ONE THING YOU CAN'T TAKE AWAY FROM ME IS THE WAY I CHOOSE TO RESPOND TO WHAT YOU DO TO ME. THE LAST OF ONE'S FREEDOMS IS TO CHOOSE ONE'S ATTITUDE IN ANY GIVEN CIRCUMSTANCE."
>
> –VIKTOR FRANKL

My treatment was set to begin with several months of chemo, followed by a month of radiation treatments. Much to my surprise, when sitting in that chemo chair for the very first time, my best friend, Fred, walked in the room. He had come to be there with me. How do you quantify friendship such as this?

During my treatment process, I encountered many folks with far worse conditions and a much graver prognosis than my own. Life had found a way of quickly putting things into proper perspective. So much so that when people at work would come into my office to tell me they had a problem, my first thought was, **"No, you don't know what a real problem is."**

These folks I met who had much tougher diagnoses than my own, became my heroes and offered me true inspiration. Their attitudes demonstrated they had chosen to live life victoriously, even if their life's duration might be a matter of weeks or months. As one friend once told me, **"Every day's a holiday and every meal's a picnic."**

With early detection, the wisdom of great doctors, loving support from my family and friends, and overwhelming strength that can be only found in God in times like this, I was very fortunate to beat that cancer. I am pleased to report that I've been cancer free ever since the end of those first chemo treatments.

62   **When circumstances, people or an illness threaten to get you down, remember you always have a choice in how you react and deal with the situation.** Choose to confront challenges head on, no matter how serious they are. And choose your friends along the way wisely, too. They'll be there for you just when you need them; supporting and encouraging you to choose to lead a powerful life—one of a Victor!

SOME QUESTIONS
TO ASK YOURSELF:

→ What challenges are you facing today?

→ Is your attitude a powerful match for them?

→ Who is your hero in life?

63

IF YOU CAN'T CHANGE IT,
CHANGE THE WAY YOU THINK ABOUT IT."
-MARY ENGELBREIT

RULE

DISCOVER YOUR MAGNETISM

"Plant the seed of desire in your mind and it forms a nucleus with power to attract to itself everything needed for its fulfillment."

— ROBERT COLLIER

A magnet serves its purpose very well. It doesn't care exactly what it attracts. It's on auto pilot and simply does its job. When we recognize that we, too, are magnets who attract people and things into our lives, we unleash the power to choose who and what we truly want to draw into our lives.

68

"WHEN WE ARE GRATEFUL FOR THE GOOD WE ALREADY HAVE, WE ATTRACT MORE GOOD INTO OUR LIFE..."

-MARGARET STORTZ

Look around you. Who and what is in your life? Whoever and whatever you find, you've attracted. That's right. You brought them all to you. You're a magnet and quite a powerful one at that.

Your thoughts, conversations and actions have drawn everything and everyone to you just like a magnet attracts metal. Do you like what you see around you in your business, your job or personal life? Well, it's all because of you.

You didn't realize you had such a strong gravitational force, did you? Like it or not, you've pulled all these people and things into your pathway to the future. Do you want to keep them along for the ride?

If you're like me, while growing up you may have often heard

"WHEN WE CREATE SOMETHING,
**WE ALWAYS CREATE FIRST
IN A THOUGHT FORM.**
IF WE ARE BASICALLY POSITIVE IN ATTITUDE,
EXPECTING AND ENVISIONING PLEASURE, SATISFACTION AND
HAPPINESS, WE WILL ATTRACT AND CREATE
PEOPLE, SITUATIONS AND EVENTS WHICH CONFORM
TO OUR POSITIVE EXPECTATIONS."

–SHAKTI GAWAIN

your parents telling you something like, "You are who you have around you. Choose your friends and associates carefully." As a child growing up, those words did not have as much meaning and significance as they do to me today. Looking back on my life, I have been fortunate to have a number of people who positively influenced my life.

71

From the cancer victors, to my friend, Fred, to exceptional business folks like Rick, John, George and my executive coach, Tony Smith, who all helped me light up the scoreboard in business and friendship, I now know they didn't just happen to come into my life. My attitude, my

> "IF YOU HAVE ZEST AND ENTHUSIASM YOU ATTRACT ZEST AND ENTHUSIASM. LIFE DOES GIVE BACK IN KIND."
>
> -NORMAN VINCENT PEALE

conversations and my way of being attracted them all to me.

Discover your magnetism and choose carefully what you say, what you think and what you do. Attract those people and things that will carry you forward to a desired state, one you truly deserve and choose to achieve—no matter what.

SOME QUESTIONS
TO ASK YOURSELF:

→ Who or what are you attracting in your life?

→ As new people enter your life, how are they the same or different than others?

→ Are your thoughts and conversations drawing powerful, positive influencers to you?

RULE # 8

GET OUTDOORS

"In wilderness I sense the miracle of life, and behind it our scientific accomplishments fade to trivia."

— CHARLES A. LINDBERGH

The great outdoors provides more than just beautiful scenery and a wealth of raw materials. Its true riches have been known for centuries. When we get outdoors, we can draw on these riches to guide us through whatever comes our way.

"I BELIEVE THAT THERE IS A SUBTLE MAGNETISM IN NATURE, WHICH, IF WE UNCONSCIOUSLY YIELD TO IT, WILL DIRECT US ARIGHT."

-HENRY DAVID THOREAU

During the course of my career, I've had the pleasure of getting to know and learn from many wonderful people from all walks of life and backgrounds. From auto mechanics, one-room school house teachers, gas station attendants and owners, outdoor power equipment dealers and service technicians, CEOs, race car drivers, team owners, authors and leading politicians, I've absorbed a wealth of knowledge and new ideas.

A meeting I had with someone who was going to do a marketing project with my company, opened my eyes to a fact I had never come across. Yet having grown up on a farm, it was always right there before my eyes.

Tina Vindum is an outdoor fitness expert and author of the book, *Tina Vindum's Outdoor Fitness*. She teaches exercise train-

"LOOK DEEP INTO NATURE, AND
THEN YOU WILL UNDERSTAND
EVERYTHING BETTER."

-ALBERT EINSTEIN

78

ers, as well as her clients, to take their fitness regimens outdoors

for improved results, both physically and mentally. When I met

Tina for the first time, she shared what is referred to as the "bio-

philia affect." **Scientists discovered that, as human beings, we**

not only crave, but have an innate need for the great outdoors.

Nature has a natural healing effect on us and serves as a natural

stress reliever. It's therefore no accident that we subconsciously fill our homes with plants or flowers or help ourselves

to fall asleep by listening to trickling brooks or the sound of rain

on sleep machines.

Tina shared with me the results

of a scientific study where **people**

in hospitals who had windows in   79

their rooms often healed faster.

In another study, scientists studied

drivers with road rage and discov-

ered that the smell of freshly-cut

grass decreased the blood pressure

of stress-filled subjects.

"EVERYBODY NEEDS BEAUTY AS WELL AS BREAD, PLACES TO PLAY IN AND PRAY IN, WHERE NATURE MAY HEAL AND CHEER AND GIVE STRENGTH TO BODY AND SOUL."

-JOHN MUIR

In our challenging world, nature provides us with an opportunity for healing and calming when you take your cares outdoors, breathe in fresh air, walk among tall trees and lift your eyes upward. You will quickly realize that no matter what obstacles you are facing, you and your worries are only a small part of the greater universe designed by our Creator. So, get yourself outdoors and on the road to rejuvenation in body and spirit. And while you're out there, focus on the present. Listen for the birds singing. No matter what the weather, they are always rejoicing!

SOME QUESTIONS
TO ASK YOURSELF:

→ How much time each day do you spend enjoying the outdoors?

→ While you are outside, are you tuning in to hear the birds singing?

→ Do you have rooms with a view? Are you bringing nature inside your home or office (i.e. live plants, fountains etc.) to create a serene environment?

81

"CLIMB UP ON SOME
HILL AT SUNRISE.
EVERYBODY NEEDS PERSPECTIVE ONCE IN A WHILE,
AND YOU'LL FIND IT THERE."
-ROBB SAGENDORPH

RULE # 9

BE LESS "IF-FY"

"If only. Those must be the two saddest words in the world."

— MERCEDES LACKEY

Life is lived here and now. Often, we already have what we need, yet we look right past it hoping for something else to come our way...

"WHEN ONE DOOR CLOSES, ANOTHER OPENS; BUT WE OFTEN LOOK SO LONG AND SO REGRETFULLY UPON THE CLOSED DOOR THAT WE DO NOT SEE THE ONE WHICH HAS OPENED FOR US."

-ALEXANDER GRAHAM BELL

Our wonderful country has afforded many of us exceptional opportunities to achieve and acquire many things. Yet, we constantly hear stories of people who are extremely accomplished in life and have many riches or opportunities, but who are very unhappy people. How can that be? A common thought is that riches will bring you happiness. If I only had more money, if I 87 could own a house, or if I only had a bigger house, a bigger/better job, a nicer car, if, if, if...

It's just a two letter word, but one that stops our growth and holds us back. When we "if" our lives away, we are giving away our power. We create a reason, an excuse for why we are not happy, fulfilled, and enriched with what we have today.

There are countless examples of people who spend part of their paycheck each week trying to win the lottery. They're looking for that ticket to win themselves a totally carefree, happy life. Yet, how many times do these big lottery winners appear in the local papers a year or two later saying how they lost their house, their spouse, their friends and that their whole life is ruined? We hear them stating, "If only I had not won that lottery!"

> "NEVER REGRET.
> IF IT'S GOOD,
> IT'S WONDERFUL.
> IF IT'S BAD,
> IT'S EXPERIENCE."
>
> -VICTORIA HOLT

When we have an "If-fy" perspective on life, we choose to ride down a road filled with "stop signs," rather than enjoying our present. You are stopped and can't move

"MOST OF US
SPEND OUR LIVES
AS IF WE HAD ANOTHER ONE
IN THE BANK."

−BEN IRWIN

forward when "If Only" starts your day.

Choose to start living in the present and you will suddenly realize the only signs around you are all saying, "Go!"

"LIVE WITH INTEN-
TION. WALK TO THE
EDGE. LISTEN HARD.
PRACTICE WELLNESS.
PLAY WITH ABANDON.
LAUGH. CHOOSE WITH
NO REGRET. APPRECI-
ATE YOUR FRIENDS.
CONTINUE TO LEARN.
DO WHAT YOU LOVE.
LIVE AS IF THIS IS
ALL THERE IS."

-MARY ANNE RADMACHER

SOME QUESTIONS
TO ASK YOURSELF:

→ Who and what are you most grateful for in your life?

→ What have you accomplished, or what have you attained that you never imagined you would ever have or achieve?

→ Are you missing out on enjoying what's happening in the present by wishing "if only" somebody or something else would come your way?

RULE # 10

MAKE IT A PURPOSE
TO KNOW YOUR
PURPOSE

"The purpose of life is a life of purpose."

– ROBERT BYRNE

*B*efore we know it, we are often flowing aimlessly down the river of life. We've left home without a map and our boat has no rudder. Consider where that journey may ultimately lead us if we choose to live our lives "on purpose..."

94

"WHEN A MAN DOES NOT
KNOW WHAT HARBOR HE
IS MAKING FOR, NO WIND
IS THE RIGHT WIND."

–SENECA

My good friend and author, Kevin McCarthy, wrote two books titled, *The On-Purpose Person* and *The On-Purpose Business*. They have both been a key component of my business and personal life. In fact, every new vendor and every new employee I met with in the past ten years received a copy of these books from me.

In *The On-Purpose Person*, Kevin artfully illustrates how each of us has a unique purpose in life. Our purpose is our heart and soul. It's who we are and why we exist. When we are "on-purpose" we are at our best, we are in the zone; we feel energized. We have meaning. When we are off-purpose, we can become stressed.

"HERE IS THE TEST TO FIND WHETHER YOUR MISSION ON EARTH IS FINISHED. IF YOU'RE ALIVE, IT ISN'T."

-RICHARD BACH

The book tells the tale of a person in search of his purpose in life. He meets with a series of mentors who each give him a bit of help along the way to discovering his purpose. It's a soulful book that makes us realize that we each have the power to become a "navigator" instead of a "floater" and chart our course in life mapped out around our own, true purpose.

96

> "HOW WE SPEND OUR DAYS IS, OF COURSE, HOW WE SPEND OUR LIVES."
>
> –ANNIE DILLARD

Make it a purpose to discover and live your purpose. Life will start to take on new meaning and become one that touches, moves and inspires not only you, but many others around you.

SOME QUESTIONS
TO ASK YOURSELF:

→ If you were designed for a reason, what do you think your unique role is?

→ What are you truly passionate about? What lights you up?

→ Do you have a mentor who helps guide you in your work or personal life?

"THE WAY YOU GET MEANING INTO YOUR LIFE IS TO
DEVOTE YOURSELF
TO LOVING OTHERS, DEVOTE YOURSELF
TO YOUR COMMUNITY AROUND YOU,
AND DEVOTE YOURSELF TO CREATING
SOMETHING THAT GIVES YOU
PURPOSE AND MEANING."
-MITCH ALBOM

FINALLY...

SLOW DOWN TO GO FASTER

*"Stress is the trash of modern life—
we all generate it but if you don't
dispose of it properly, it will pile up
and overtake your life."*

—TERRI GUILLEMETS

There's a saying in NASCAR® that sometimes you have to slow down in order to go fast. In this complicated, fast-paced world of cell phones, the Internet, iPods®, iPads®, and Smart phones, do you find it difficult to slow down? Sometimes life intervenes and does the "slowing" for us—whether it's an illness, job loss or the loss of a loved one. We often don't slow down by choice.

102

If we never slow down, we may never take notice of the little things hiding out in the rocks high above, we may never fully take notice of who and what is in our lives and how powerfully magnetic we are. **By slowing down we can take time to discover our purpose and choose to fully live it each and every day.**

Before something else intervenes on your behalf, choose to slow down. Take that vacation you've always wanted to take. Go back to school and learn a new trade or complete your degree. Downsize that big house to something you can really afford. Read the job postings and go for that new career or job you always wished for.

Making a move to the right hand lane may make you think things and life are going to pass you by. Yet, choosing to slow

> "HALF OUR LIFE IS SPENT TRYING TO FIND SOMETHING TO DO WITH THE TIME WE HAVE RUSHED THROUGH LIFE TRYING TO SAVE."
>
> —WILL ROGERS

down not only lets us enjoy the road along the way, it can supercharge us to reach our ultimate destination.

Life is meant to be enjoyed and lived fully. Allowing stress to take over is a choice that's completely in our control. Things happen in our lives, but it's our attitude toward them that will make all the difference. Make a choice to stop being a stress magnet and instead attract a simplified way of being.

Talk to others who have simplified and ask them how they have achieved it. Reduce the numbers, look for what's missing and leave your past behind.

Ready to get out that blank sheet of paper? Whatever it is you want to attract or put into your life, start with your thoughts. If **"we become what we think about,"** what will you choose to become? Who will you choose to surround yourself with? Find others who will support you and who are also committed to simplifying. What conversations do you need to have with them?

105

Start the process to slow down in order to win the race, and you will discover that stress is a choice, indeed.

"THERE IS MORE TO LIFE THAN INCREASING ITS SPEED."

-MAHATMA GANDHI

"**SLOW DOWN**
AND EVERYTHING YOU
ARE CHASING WILL COME AROUND
AND **CATCH YOU.**"

-JOHN DE PAOLA

About the Author

A leader who has an innate talent to touch, move and inspire others, Dave Zerfoss lives his purpose which is "empowering others to create powerful futures." An accomplished business professional who is highly skilled in transformational leadership, executive coaching and public speaking, Zerfoss connects with people from all walks of life. He draws on personal life examples, from growing up on a farm in rural Pennsylvania where he attended a one-room school house, to achieving hundreds of millions of dollars in sales increases during his 18-year tenure as President of Husqvarna Professional Products, Inc.

A down-to-earth individual, yet one who believes in big ideas and bold declarations, Dave leads the Zerfoss Group which consults with "think tanks," major corporations and entrepreneurs. As an Executive in Residence at Queens University McColl School of Business in Charlotte, North Carolina, he enjoys sharing transformational thinking and leadership insights with aspiring MBA and Executive MBA students. Dave is also living his purpose as he Chairs a chief executive group for Vistage International. He resides in Davidson, North Carolina with his wife, Barbara.

Dave invites your thoughts. He can be reached at
www.TheZerfossGroup.com

If you have enjoyed this book we invite you to check out
our entire collection of gift books, with free inspirational movies,
at www.simpletruths.com. You'll discover it's a great way to inspire friends
and family, or to thank your best customers and employees.

FOR MORE INFORMATION, PLEASE VISIT US AT:
WWW.SIMPLETRUTHS.COM OR CALL US TOLL FREE...
800-900-3427